THE ROAD RAGE
CURE FOR YOUNG DRIVERS

A Roadmap to Clarity, Humility and a Peaceful Life

DR. MORT ORMAN, M.D.
Leading Anger Elimination Expert

Copyright © 2025 by Morton C. Orman, M.D.
All rights reserved.

Except as permitted under the U.S. copyright Act of 1976, no part of this publication may be reproduced, distributed, or transmitted in any form or by any means, or stored in a database or retrieval system, without the prior written permission of the publisher.

Published by:
TRO Productions, LLC
Sebastian, Florida 32958

Paperback ISBN: 978-1-886660-09-0
Hardcover ISBN: 978-1-886660-08-3
ebook ISBN: 978-1-886660-10-6

Disclaimers and Legal Notices

Both the author and publisher of this book have strived to be as accurate as possible in this informational product. While all attempts have been made to verify the information herein, there is no warranty either expressly stated or implied of complete or permanent accuracy, as knowledge does evolve and change.

The author, publisher, and any subsequent distributors of this work assume no responsibility for any errors, assumptions, or interpretations made as result of consuming this information. The reader is solely responsible for how he/she chooses to understand and/or make use of this information.

Please use prudent judgment in attempting to apply any strategies, exercises, or other recommendations suggested herein. Any perceived slights of specific persons, peoples, or organizations are unintentional.

This book is not intended as substitute for professional medical or psychological advice or treatment when these may be needed. If medical, psychological, or other expert advice or treatment is needed, the services of an appropriate professional should be sought.

If you suffer from very severe anxiety, severe phobias, severe depression or any other serious mental health condition, the advice in this book may not be appropriate or sufficient for you. If you are not already doing so, you are hereby advised to consult and work with an experienced mental health professional.

If you believe that your symptoms or your problems are beginning to get worse as you read this book, stop reading it immediately and consult a trained health professional.

Dr. Mort Orman is a board-certified Internal Medicine physician. As a medical professional, he has successfully helped and coached people to overcome their anger, stress and anxiety related problems for more than 40 years. However, he is not a licensed nor a practicing mental health professional. As such, each individual needs to personally assess and evaluate all suggestions and advice noted in this book.

Bottom line: you are 100% responsible for how you interpret and make use of the information in this book. So please do so wisely.

Selected Other Books by Doc Orman

Stress Relief Wisdom:
Ten Key Distinctions For A Stress Free Life

The Choice Of Paradox: *How "Opposite Thinking" Can Improve Your Life and Reduce Your Stress*

Stop Negative Thinking:
How To Stop Worrying, Relieve Stress, and Become a Happy Person Again

The Irritability Cure:
How To Stop Being Angry, Anxious and Frustrated All the Time

The Art Of True Forgiveness:
How To Forgive Anyone For Anything, Anytime You Want

The Test Anxiety Cure:
How To Overcome Exam Anxiety, Fear and Self Defeating Habits

The Panic Attack Solution:
How To Stop Panic Attacks, Anxiety and Stress For Good

The 14 Day Stress Cure: *A New Approach For Dealing With Stress That Can Change Your Life*

Dr. Orman's Life Changing Anger Cure:
Eliminate Unwanted Anger, Without Anger Management, So You Can Be Happier, Healthier, and Don't End Up Alone

FREE DOWNLOADABLE GIFT

Thank you for checking out this book on how young drivers can eliminate road rage and other forms of unwanted, harmful anger from their life.

If you would like more information on how to better understand and deal with anger, whether related to the roads or not, please download my free PDF guide, *"The Best Anger Elimination Method You Can Find."*

Here is the link:

http://TheAngerSolution.org

Click on the link, enter your first name and best email, and the guide will arrive in your email inbox within 10 minutes time.

Dedication

To every young driver who has ever felt their heartbeat thunder at a red light, palms grip the wheel in frustration, or anger directed at other drivers flare up suddenly—this book is for you. May these pages guide you toward calmness behind the wheel, courage to face your frustrations, and the freedom that comes from choosing compassion over rage. You're not alone in this journey; each mile you drive can be a step toward greater understanding—both of fellow travelers on the road and a deeper and more powerful understanding of yourself.

Note To Readers

This book is one of three similar books about how to end the problem of road rage for various types of drivers. These include:

The Road Rage Cure For Young Drivers
The Road Rage Cure For Parents
The Road Rage Cure For Professional Drivers and Commuters

All three books share the same subtitle: *A Roadmap to Clarity, Humility and a Peaceful Life.* That's because each book presents the same basic insights and cure for road rage, gained through clarity, humility, and telling the truth about what's really happening when we get triggered to become angry.

> **IMPORTANT: You only need to read one of these books.**

Grab the one that speaks to you most directly and start reading. They all lead to the same destination—how to let go of road rage and discover the secrets of having a peaceful and rewarding anger-free life.

The important thing to appreciate about road rage is that it's not about the road or other drivers. It is ultimately about YOU! It's about how you live your life, how you perceive reality, how well you understand yourself, how well you know what is causing your anger (and other emotions) to occur, and how well you relate to and respect other human beings.

Whichever book you choose, if you read it seriously with the intention to see things differently and learn something new, you will grow by leaps and bounds in all of these important dimensions.

Trust me, if you rage on the road, you may rage in many other areas of your life. And repeatedly getting angry will eventually cost you . . . big time! So, it's time to put your road rage in the rearview mirror and learn how to be wiser, more truthful, and much more compassionate and forgiving to your fellow human beings.

Welcome to one of the most rewarding journeys you could ever embark on . . . learning to eliminate road rage and other forms of unwanted anger from your life . . . once and for all.

Table of Contents

Note to Readers vii

Chapter 1
Younger Drivers Are Different Than Older Drivers. 1

Chapter 2
The Prevalence of Road Rage in Young Drivers. 5

Chapter 3
The Cost of Road Rage to Young Drivers and Society 9

Chapter 4
Why Most Approaches to Curbing Road Rage Don't Work . . . 13

Chapter 5
What Is Needed for Young Drivers to Stop Raging
on the Road 19

Chapter 6
Common Misconceptions About the Causes of Road Rage . . 25

Chapter 7
The Real (But Invisible) Internal Causes of Road Rage 31

Chapter 8
The Ultimate Cause of Road Rage In All Human Drivers. . . . 37

Chapter 9
Here's the Cure (WARNING: TOUGH LOVE AHEAD) 45

Chapter 10
You Are Not as Smart as You Think You Are
(Tough Love Part 2). 53

Table of Contents - continued

Chapter 11
You Are Not as Right as You Think and Feel You Are
(Tough Love Part 3).................................. 59

Chapter 12
Three Ways Your Brain Is Tricking You
When You Get Angry................................. 65

Chapter 13
A Window Into the Truth About Anger 73

Chapter 14
Inner Peace Through Humility, Honesty, and Clarity 79

Chapter 15
Putting It All Together: Implementing the Cure........... 85

Chapter 16
Summary, Conclusions and Next Steps 91

Epilogue 95

Appendix A: Common Road Rage Triggers 97

Appendix B: Examples of Telling the Truth 104

About the Author.................................. 109

CHAPTER I

Young Drivers Are Different Than Older Drivers

Freedom feels endless when you grip the steering wheel for the first time as a new driver. You're in control—at least, that's what you tell yourself. For young drivers, the road represents speed, power, and adventure. But with that newfound independence often comes something else: impatience, frustration, and an inability to recognize that you aren't yet as calm, controlled, or unshakeable as you think.

Young drivers are not just less experienced; their brains are wired differently. Science shows that a young driver's emotional impulses, risk perception, and decision-making are all still under construction. This gap between confidence and actual wisdom can fuel a perfect storm for road rage—an invisible ticking bomb ready to ignite in response to a simple honk, a slow driver, or a perceived slight.

The Biological Difference

Young drivers are in a rapid brain development phase, particularly in the prefrontal cortex—the area responsible for decision-making and impulse control. This means that as a young driver, when you encounter challenges or obstacles on the road, you are more likely to react emotionally, rather than rationally. Coupled with a surge of hormones and a tendency toward risk-taking behaviors, the deck is stacked against you when trying to maintain emotional and behavioral control during stressful situations.

The Social and Cultural Influences

In addition to biology, societal expectations and peer influences also play a significant role in road rage for young drivers. Many young men, for example, feel socially pressured to assert dominance or maintain an image of toughness, especially in confrontational scenarios like road incidents. Though rarely acknowledged, this mindset amplifies the likelihood of aggressive driving behaviors.

Now that young women are being encouraged to be more strong, independent and assertive when they get behind the wheel, they too might be socially influenced to "do everything men can do," especially when it comes to road rage behaviors.

Also, there seems to be a prevalent social mindset among young and older drivers that "bad" drivers, "slow" drivers, and "inconsiderate" drivers need to be punished for their less than optimal driving behaviors. This often fuels various expressions of road rage, as enraged drivers believe—either consciously or unconsciously—that they are doing something positive for society by delivering the required punitive consequences.

Understanding the Emotional Triggers

For young and older drivers, road rage often stems from deeper internal triggers such as feeling disrespected, hassled, or inconvenienced by others on the road. These moments tap into a reservoir of frustration and insecurity, often unrelated to driving itself. For example, a bad day at work or unresolved family tensions can manifest as an angry outburst when someone cuts you off in heavy traffic.

The Ripple Effects of Road Rage

Also, the consequences of road rage for drivers of all ages go far beyond the momentary release of anger. Road rage can lead to reckless driving, accidents, strained relationships, and even long-term health issues like high blood pressure or chronic stress.

As a young driver, you may not have the experience yet to appreciate how chronic anger, frustration, and stress can adversely affect your health as you age. But as a physician, I can tell you that it certainly does. Hopefully, by understanding these and other risks to your future well-being, you can begin to see the importance of addressing your anger now—not just on the road but in every area of your life.

A Call to Awareness

This chapter sets the stage for the transformative journey that lies directly ahead. By recognizing the unique challenges you face as a young driver and gaining more insights into the underlying factors fueling your road rage, you can take the first steps toward lasting change. The path to calm, unflappable driving and a calmer life in general starts with increased awareness—and this awareness begins now.

CHAPTER 2

The Prevalence of Road Rage in Young Drivers

Road rage isn't just a rare occurrence—it's a widespread phenomenon, especially among young drivers. If you think only you or a handful of others struggle with uncontrollable anger behind the wheel, think again. Studies show that young men between the ages of 16 and 30 are significantly more likely to experience and act out road rage than any other demographic group. But why is this so common, and what does it reveal about the modern driving experience for young people?

The Alarming Statistics

Recent research shows that nearly 80% of drivers admit to experiencing road rage at least once a month, with young drivers ranking at the top. Aggressive behaviors like tailgating, yelling, honking excessively, and weaving through traffic are more frequently reported among young men than young women or older drivers. In some cases, minor incidents have escalated into physical confrontations or accidents with life-changing consequences.

Real-Life Stories

Take the case of Jake, a 19-year-old college student who was late for class and in a hurry when another driver cut him off. Overwhelmed by frustration, Jake sped up, honked his horn repeatedly, and ended up in a dangerous game of cat and mouse on the highway. The result? A minor collision that could have been avoided and hundreds of dollars in repair costs. Jake's story isn't unique—it's a sobering example of how quickly emotions on the road can spiral out of control.

Why Young Drivers Are More Susceptible

Young drivers face a combination of pressures that make road rage more likely:

- **Stress and Anxiety:** From school pressures to jobs, young men and women often juggle multiple responsibilities that heighten stress levels.

- **Overconfidence:** Many young drivers overestimate their abilities and underestimate risks, which can lead to problems when things don't go as planned.

- **Impatience:** The desire to reach a destination quickly or "win" on the road fuels impulsive and risky behaviors.

- **Expectations:** Believing that others should never impede your progress, never drive faster or slower than you, and never get angry at you on the road is a formula for disappointment, anger, and chronic resentment.

The Societal Cost of Road Rage

Road rage doesn't just affect you, the driver—it impacts everyone. Accidents caused by aggressive driving cost billions annually in medical expenses, repairs, insurance payouts, and lost productivity. More importantly, they cause emotional devastation for families who lose loved ones in preventable collisions.

The increase of anger-prone drivers on the road makes the entire driving experience more tense, combative, and anxiety producing for everyone.

The First Step: Acknowledgment

Recognizing the prevalence of road rage among young drivers is the first important step. It's not about assigning blame—it's about understanding the problem.

You are not alone. You are also not beyond help. By acknowledging how widespread road rage is and the factors that fuel it, you're already on the path to overcoming it. This book will guide you step by step, but it starts with a simple truth: road rage is common, especially for young drivers, but it doesn't have to define you. And you don't have to continue suffering from it or struggling with it. You can get rid of it, and this book will show you how.

"The effects of road rage don't stop when you park your car. Anger on the road often spills into personal relationships, leading to conflicts with family, friends, and partners."

CHAPTER 3

The Cost of Road Rage to Young Drivers and Society

Every time anger takes over behind the wheel, it comes with a cost. For young drivers, the price of road rage often stretches far beyond the immediate moment of frustration and triggered emotions. From financial penalties to emotional scars and even irreversible tragedies, the ripple effects of aggressive driving can impact lives in profound ways.

Personal Costs: More Than Just a Fine

For young drivers, a moment of rage can quickly lead to expensive consequences. Speeding tickets, increased insurance premiums, and vehicle repairs are just the beginning. More serious incidents, like reckless driving charges or at-fault accidents, can result in court fees, community service, and even jail time. And let's not forget the intangible toll—the guilt and regret that linger long after a heated encounter on the road or especially if your anger leads to injury, disability, or the death of others.

Health Consequences

Road rage isn't just destructive for your driving record; it's terrible for your health. Frequent episodes of anger can lead to chronic stress, high blood pressure, and an increased risk of heart disease. For young men who already face societal pressures and personal challenges, the added burden of poor health can create a cycle of frustration that's hard to break.

Impact on Relationships

The effects of road rage don't stop when you park your car. Anger on the road often spills into personal relationships, leading to conflicts with family, friends, and partners. Young drivers who struggle with emotional control may find themselves isolated, misunderstood, and at odds with the people they care about most.

The Societal Price Tag

Aggressive driving isn't just an individual problem—it's a societal one. Road rage-related accidents account for billions of dollars in medical costs, property damage, and lost productivity annually. Emergency responders, insurance companies, and employers all bear the burden of these preventable incidents, creating a ripple effect that touches every corner of society.

A New Perspective on Accountability

Understanding the actual costs of road rage is a wake-up call. It's not just about avoiding a ticket or keeping your car in one piece—it's about recognizing how your actions affect yourself, your loved ones, and the world around you. You can break the cycle and create a safer, calmer environment for everyone by taking accountability for your emotions and your actions. As you read along in this book, I'll show you exactly how to do this.

In these first few chapters, we've briefly addressed the far-reaching consequences of personal and societal road rage. However, knowing the cost is only the first step. In the next chapter, we'll explore why traditional approaches to managing road rage fall short—and soon after that you will see what truly works to address the root causes.

*"Anger isn't just about the external trigger—
it's about how the external trigger activates
(i.e., triggers) other anger-generating causes within us."*

CHAPTER 4

Why Most Approaches to Curbing Road Rage Don't Work

Experts and self-help gurus have offered solutions to curb road rage for years. These methods often include deep breathing exercises, counting to ten, or listening to calming music. While these and other anger management techniques might provide temporary relief, they fail to address the **root causes** of excessive anger behind the wheel. Thus, most approaches focus on temporarily managing anger rather than permanently eliminating it entirely—and this is where they fall short.

The Problem with Anger Management

The term "anger management" has become a popular buzzword today. It is usually regarded as the ideal way to deal with anger problems, large and small. However, the fundamental premise of anger management is seriously flawed.

Managing anger assumes that it's a natural emotion that arises from external events that can't be avoided or eliminated and therefore our anger must be controlled. However, this approach ignores that anger is often a learned response generated primarily by **internal causes**, not external situations or events. Instead of addressing why anger arises so easily from factors inside us, anger management strategies simply teach individuals how to cope by focusing mainly on reducing symptoms while ignoring the more important internal causes.

Temporary Fixes vs. Lasting Change

Techniques like counting to ten or taking deep breaths are akin to putting a band-aid on a wound that requires stitches. These methods might defuse immediate anger but don't prevent it from bubbling up again the next time a stressful situation arises. Lasting change requires a deeper understanding not just of the external triggers (usually obvious to all) but also of the invisible internal causes that give rise to our anger and fuel it to escalate (you'll learn about these invisible causes later in this book).

Why Calming Music Isn't Enough

Many drivers have been advised to listen to calming music or podcasts to reduce stress while driving. While this can create a soothing environment, it's not a cure-all. When an external trigger occurs, such as being cut off in traffic, the calming effect of the music often dissipates. True emotional control comes from within, not external distractions or other anger management techniques.

The Danger of Suppression

Another common tactic is to suppress anger. Drivers are told to "suck it up" or "stay calm at all costs." However, suppression can lead to internalized stress, which manifests as tension, anxiety, or even physical health problems. Suppressing anger without addressing its root causes is like trying to keep a lid on a boiling pot—eventually, it will overflow.

The Missing Piece: Understanding Root Causes

The key to overcoming road rage lies in understanding its invisible internal root causes.

Anger isn't just about the external trigger—it's about how the external trigger activates (i.e., triggers) other anger-generating causes within us. For instance, being cut off in traffic might make one driver furious while another is hardly annoyed. In both situations, the external cause is exactly the same. So, the external cause alone cannot be the whole story.

The difference in who experiences anger or road rage and who does not comes down to internal beliefs, expectations, perceptual styles, and other internal factors that shape how individuals react to events.

Shifting the Focus from Reaction to Prevention

Instead of teaching drivers how to behave less aggressively or "manage" their anger, we must teach them how to prevent or quickly abort aggressive, angry reactions altogether. This involves:

- **Identifying External and Internal Triggers:** Recognizing specific situations along with specific internal thoughts and beliefs igniting anger.

- **Challenging Beliefs:** Questioning the internal narratives that fuel frustration, anger, and road rage, such as "People should never disrespect me," "I have to be in control at all times," or "How dare they drive that way."

- **Developing Emotional Awareness:** Learning to notice the early signs of anger in your body and addressing them quickly and effectively before they escalate.

- **True Emotional Intelligence:** Understanding the invisible internal causes of human anger so you can recall them from memory every single time you become angry, on the road or anywhere else! I'll show you how to do this shortly. In fact, one of the primary goals of this book is to show you this is not hard to do, and it is much easier and simpler than most people, including many emotions experts, currently appreciate.

A Call for a New Approach

This chapter exposes the shortcomings of traditional anger management strategies and highlights the need for a new, transformative approach. By shifting the focus from managing anger to better understanding how it is generated within you, you can learn how to eliminate it quickly and easily, thereby achieving true emotional mastery.

The journey won't be easy, but the rewards—peaceful drives, healthier relationships, and a calmer mind—are well worth the effort.

WHY MOST APPROACHES TO CURBING ROAD RAGE DON'T WORK

Let me ask you this: If there were a way you could learn how to quickly abort or eliminate your angry reactions whenever they occur, would that be of interest to you? I believe most people, regardless of age, would love to have this skill, because we all know that unwanted anger can be enormously harmful to our lives.

You're in luck. There is a way to eliminate and not manage your angry reactions whenever you want. And this is what makes this book, and my two other Road Rage Cure books just like it, different from almost every other book about road rage that has ever been written.

In the next chapter, we'll explore the mindset shifts and practical tools needed for young drivers to stop raging on the road and start driving with confidence, calm, and clarity.

"Ending road rage isn't just about keeping your temper in check... It's about understanding yourself more deeply as a human being and expanding your insights about where anger originates from inside your brain and body."

CHAPTER 5

What Is Needed for Young Drivers to Stop Raging on the Road

Ending road rage isn't just about keeping your temper in check; it's about making fundamental changes in your mindset and behaviors. It's about understanding yourself more deeply as a human being and expanding your insights about where anger originates from inside your brain and body.

As we've already established, young drivers face unique challenges, from heightened emotional responses to societal pressures that often glorify anger displays and aggression. To stop raging on the road, young drivers need a combination of deeper self-awareness, anger elimination insights, anger elimination skills, and a new approach to understanding how anger gets created for all human beings, young and old.

Mindset Shifts for Calm Driving

The first step to ending road rage is rethinking what it means to be a successful driver. Many young drivers equate driving with dominance, speed, and competition. Instead, you can decide for yourself to define success as reaching your destination safely, feeling calm, remaining relaxed and in control, and both respecting and forgiving others on the road.

1. **Embrace Patience as a Strength:** Recognize that patience is not a weakness but a skill that reflects maturity, wisdom, and personal control.

2. **Shift the Focus from Others to Yourself:** Instead of blaming other drivers for perceived slights or misdeeds on the road, focus on how your own brain has automatically caused you to judge other drivers critically, whether they truly deserve those judgments or not.

3. **Redefine Winning:** Winning isn't about being the fastest, the angriest, or the most assertive; it's about avoiding conflict, knowing how to abort your angry reactions quickly, and staying composed, loving, and compassionate to your fellow drivers on the road.

Practical "Management" Tools to Stay Calm

Once these mindset changes are in place, which often takes time and practice, drivers can also benefit from specific anger management strategies they can use in real time to prevent anger from escalating.

1. **Pre-Drive Rituals:** Before starting the car, take a few moments to set an intention for a calm and safe drive. Visualize arriving at your destination feeling good about your experience.

2. **Controlled Breathing:** When stress arises, use deep breathing techniques to calm your nervous system and refocus your energy.

3. **Anchoring Techniques:** Repeat a calming phrase, such as "I am in control," when you feel anger or frustration bubbling up.

4. **Creating Safe Spacing:** Think about creating a safe distance between you and the car in front of you. Value that space for protecting you and others from harm.

Note: Even though anger management techniques mainly deal with temporary symptom relief, they can still play a role, especially when you are just beginning to learn how to eliminate your anger by addressing internal root causes.

The Role of Emotional Intelligence

Emotional intelligence (EQ) plays a significant role in preventing road rage. EQ, as currently promoted, is defined as the ability to recognize, understand, and manage one's emotions—a set of skills that can be developed over time.

- **Self-Awareness:** Learn to recognize anger's physical and emotional signs before it takes over.

- **Empathy:** Try to see the road from another driver's perspective. The person who cut you off might be having an emergency or simply made an innocent mistake.

- **Impulse Control:** Practice delaying or aborting your knee-jerk, automatic angry reactions. A few seconds of reflection can prevent minutes or years of regret.

Building Healthy Habits

To make lasting changes, young drivers need to build habits that support calm driving.

- **Regular Reflection:** After each drive, reflect on what went well and what could have been handled differently. This practice helps reinforce positive behavior and recalling positive mindsets.

- **Accountability Partners:** Share your goals with a trusted friend or family member who can provide encouragement and honest feedback.

- **Consistent Practice:** Like any skill, staying calm while driving requires consistent effort and practice.

A New Vision for the Road

Imagine a world where roads and highways are places of cooperation, not competition. Where drivers respect each other's space, are understanding and forgiving of each other's minor mistakes, and everyone gets home safely.

This vision isn't just a fantasy—it's achievable when young drivers take responsibility for their actions and embrace the tools and mindsets needed to drive with clarity, calm, and confidence.

In the next chapter, we'll explore common misconceptions about the causes of road rage and how understanding what truly is causing our anger can lead to profound transformation.

Note: *The type of Advanced Emotional Intelligence you will gain from this book, about the internal causes of anger in general and road rage in particular, will put you far ahead of most other people your age with regard to controlling and eliminating your unwanted angry reactions.*

"Misconceptions about road rage run deep, and many of these false beliefs prevent drivers who want to stop getting angry on the road from addressing the real issues at play."

CHAPTER 6

Common Misconceptions About the Causes of Road Rage

In this chapter, we will begin to uncover what most people (of all ages) misunderstand about anger. The younger you are when you learn these valuable lessons, the less you will suffer from the damaging consequences anger can have throughout your lifetime.

Let's start by exposing some major myths and misconceptions about anger and its causes.

When you think of road rage, it's easy to blame external triggers: heavy traffic, a rude gesture, or a careless driver cutting you off. While these external events might spark your anger, they are not the root cause. These very common external events merely trigger specific internal causes (totally invisible to you and everyone else) inside your brain and body, which are actually the root causes of your anger. Different emotions, like fear, worry, jealousy, guilt, and sadness, are also created within us in exactly the same invisible ways.

Misconceptions about road rage run deep, and many of these false beliefs prevent drivers who want to stop getting angry on the road from addressing the real issues at play.

Myth 1: Road Rage Is Caused by Other Drivers

The biggest misconception about road rage is that other people cause it. Angry drivers often point the finger at other travelers on the road, blaming reckless or inconsiderate behavior. However, *the truth is that road rage is more about your own invisible internal reactions* than the triggering external events. Two drivers can experience the exact same situation—one might shrug it off while the other explodes in anger. This difference highlights that the real causes lie within, even if we can't see them.

Myth 2: Road Rage Is Inevitable in Heavy Traffic

Many believe that road rage is a natural response to frustrating situations like gridlock or slow-moving traffic. While these conditions can test anyone's patience, they don't inherently cause anger. The anger and frustration ultimately stem from internal factors, such as unmet expectations, the desire to reach a destination quickly, or an excessive need to avoid delays. *Learning to tell the truth about these often unrealistic expectations* can drastically reduce the likelihood of you exploding into rage.

Myth 3: Aggressive Driving Is a Necessary Response

Some drivers view aggressive behavior on the road as a way to "show" others the error of their ways or establish dominance on the road. These internal beliefs are not only misguided but also dangerous. Aggression rarely leads to better outcomes—it often escalates conflicts and increases the risk of accidents and physical harm.

Myth 4: Certain Personality Types Are Just Angry Drivers

Labeling yourself or others as "just an angry driver" or "just an angry person" is tempting, as if road rage is a fixed, unchangeable personality trait. While some personality traits, like impulsivity or competitiveness, may make anger more likely, road rage is not hardwired.

However, when you do indulge in road rage frequently over time, your brain and body do get conditioned to react with anger more easily. This type of conditioning may look and feel permanent, but it's not. With increased self-awareness and the right anger elimination insights and strategies—which you will learn from this book—even the angriest drivers can change.

Myth 5: Venting Your Anger or Frustration Helps

The idea that yelling, honking, making rude gestures, or otherwise releasing or expressing your angry feelings are good for you is a myth. Venting intensifies your emotions rather than calming them down. In addition, each angry outburst reinforces the habit of reacting angrily and possibly aggressively, making it harder to break the cycle over time.

When you focus on overtly expressing or demonstrating your anger, you are not looking inward to pinpoint and then rectify the internal causes. This is perhaps the biggest drawback to venting your anger—you never learn how to develop the internal wisdom, increased self-awareness, and increased self-control to keep your angry reactions and responses from happening repeatedly.

The Truth About Triggers

Telling the truth about road rage begins with acknowledging that the common observable triggers are just triggers. They don't create your anger; they activate existing thought patterns, *perceptual filters*, and other conditioned behaviors inside your brain and body. These internal patterns are strongly shaped by how our human brains have evolved over millions of years. They are also shaped by our past experiences, personal beliefs, and even cultural norms and attitudes about driving, judging others, masculinity, competition, time urgency, telling the truth, and many other aspects of daily life.

A Shift in Perspective

By debunking these myths, drivers of all ages can start to see road rage in a new and more accurate light. It's not so much about traffic, bad drivers, unavoidable frustrations, or other external factors—as most people mistakenly assume. It's about *internal factors* such as how you interpret and respond to challenges on the road, how your brain automatically filters your views of the world (more about this later), and how well you understand what is really going on.

COMMON MISCONCEPTIONS ABOUT THE CAUSES OF ROAD RAGE

Recognizing this primary truth about road rage—**it's an internal battle you need to wage and win**—is the first step toward gaining control and breaking free from anger.

In the next three chapters, we'll explore the real internal causes of road rage and how understanding them can lead to profound change and a liberation from anger you may not believe is possible.

*". . . the truth is that the real causes of road rage are **invisible**, rooted deep within our brains and bodies. "*

CHAPTER 7

The Real (But Invisible) Internal Causes of Road Rage

As we've already established, most drivers, regardless of age, think road rage is about what happens around and outside of them: slow traffic, reckless behavior, or something as simple as an unexpected honk. But the truth is that *the real causes of road rage are **invisible***, rooted deep within our brains and bodies. These underlying internal factors shape how we perceive and react emotionally and behaviorally to events and challenges on the road—and they're far more powerful than any external trigger.

*Once you know what these **invisible internal causes** are and you are willing to tell the truth about them, you can stop struggling with anger and learn how to emerge victorious. That's because the internal causes of our emotions are always highly susceptible to your direct personal control, whereas external situations and events are usually not.*

40 Years of Anger Elimination Success

Forty years ago, I discovered how to pinpoint the specific internal causes of anger in myself and all other human beings.

I have used this new awareness to end my own habitual road rage and eliminate most other anger from my life. I have also used it to become one of the premier anger elimination experts in the world today and to help hundreds of individuals finally surmount their own resistant anger problems.

This book does not describe all the steps I took to make this discovery forty years ago. I described the path I took in great detail in my recent comprehensive book on eliminating anger, **Dr. Orman's Life Changing Anger Cure**, released in April, 2024. If you are genuinely interested in getting rid of your road rage or any other unwanted anger in your life, I highly recommend you purchase and study this book as well. Here is the link to check it out on Amazon: http://BestAngerBook.com

In this chapter, I will summarize what **other experts** have said about the internal causes of human anger. I believe many of these causes identified and discussed by others are at least somewhat correct. However, I have found a simpler, all-inclusive framework that I will share with you in the next chapter. I will also show you how these more commonly referenced internal causes, which I highlight in this chapter, all derive from a deeper set of *only three primary internal causes*.

In other words, while it might appear there are a wide range of internal causes for human anger, as others have speculated, it turns out there are only three simple internal causes you need to understand and recall to account for them all.

Unrealistic Expectations

One of the most common invisible causes of road rage is unrealistic expectations. Many drivers who are prone to road rage assume that traffic will always flow smoothly, everyone will follow the rules, and their journey will go smoothly as planned. When reality doesn't align with these expectations, frustration and anger frequently arise.

For young drivers, who often lack the wisdom of living a long, introspective life, this gap between expectation and reality can feel particularly jarring, leading to impulsive reactions.

A Sense of Entitlement

Another commonly discussed internal cause of road rage is entitlement. Some drivers believe they deserve priority on the road, whether it's the fastest lane, the right of way, or unimpeded travel. When other drivers don't "respect" this perceived entitlement, anger flares. Recognizing and letting go of this unrealistic (i.e., false and egoistic) mindset is key to maintaining calm.

Emotional Residue from Daily Life

Anger on the road often has little to do with driving itself. Stress from school, work, unresolved arguments, or personal insecurities can create a reservoir of tension that overflows at the first sign of trouble or being inconvenienced. Thus, your car can become a vessel for venting strong emotions that have nothing to do with traffic.

Perceived Lack of Control

Driving can feel like a high-stakes activity where mistakes have serious consequences. Being cut off or stuck in gridlock can trigger a sense of helplessness for young drivers. This perceived lack of control (internal cause) often produces anger, which, in this case, is an attempt to reclaim a sense of power in an uncontrollable environment.

Cultural Influences

Society plays a role in road rage, too. In many cultures, driving is seen as a test of masculinity, dominance, or competence. These internal causes become deeply ingrained into the brains and bodies of many people who grow up in those cultures. Young men, in particular, may feel pressure to "prove" themselves or their manhood on the road. This internal mindset creates a breeding ground for aggression and conflict. We also previously discussed the "punisher" mindset, where people have been conditioned to believe it is their social role to meet out punishments on the road to those drivers who behave "inappropriately."

Unconscious Thought Patterns

Additional deeply ingrained thought patterns (internal causes) have been attributed to fueling road rage. These include beliefs, all of which are false or unrealistic, like:

- "People should always respect me on the road."
- "I have to aggressively defend myself and my loved ones from bad drivers."
- "I should always be able to get where I am going without interruptions."
- "Being late is never acceptable."
- "I don't have to leave 15 minutes early or check traffic warnings to avoid arriving late because I am so special that nothing unexpected will come up to impede my progress.

Recognizing these unconscious internal scripts is the first step to letting go and then rewriting them.

Breaking the Cycle

Understanding these and other internal causes of road rage empowers you and other young drivers to break the cycle. By identifying and addressing these invisible factors, which often get activated unconsciously and automatically, like "knee-jerk" reflexes, young drivers can consciously shift their perspectives and respond to challenges with newfound clarity and calmness.

"At its core, road rage is not about traffic, other drivers, or even the act of driving itself. It is ultimately about your brain and how it has been conditioned to respond automatically."

CHAPTER 8

The Ultimate Cause of Road Rage In All Human Drivers

Beneath all the external triggers, misconceptions about the internal causes, and strong emotional reactions we experience, there lies *one ultimate cause of road rage*. If you understand this ultimate internal cause, you can free yourself from road rage and other destructive forms of unwanted anger in your life. If you don't, you will not be able to truly eliminate road rage or any other type of anger.

Here is the ultimate cause: At its core, road rage is not about traffic, other drivers, or even the act of driving itself. **It is ultimately about your brain** and how it has been **conditioned** to respond **automatically** through millions of years of human evolution, plus all the years of experiences you have had on planet Earth.

How Invisible Processes in Your Brain Create a Chain Reaction Resulting in Anger

Most people alive today mistakenly believe anger is a two-step cause-effect process:

1. **The Trigger:** A driver cuts you off, traffic slows un-

expectedly, or someone runs a red light. (External Cause)

2. **The Emotional and Behavioral Responses:** You immediately feel angry and begin to engage in whatever behaviors you have learned to exhibit in these situations. (Internal Effects)

Thus, our conceptual model of anger generation (which also applies to all our other emotions) is that "one causes two"—end of story.

In other words, the external triggers cause us to react the way we do.

The problem with this popular model is that it is incorrect. Anger generation is actually a four-step process, not a two-step process:

1. **The Trigger:** A driver cuts you off, traffic slows unexpectedly, or someone runs a red light. (External Cause)

2. **Internal Cause 1:** This is the first internal process that occurs in your brain (not visible to you or to others)

3. **Internal Cause 2:** This is the second internal process that occurs in your brain (also not visible to you or to others)

4. **The Emotional and Behavioral Responses:** You instantly feel angry and begin to engage in whatever behaviors you have learned to exhibit in these situations. (Internal Effects)

In other words, anger generation is a 1-2-3-4 sequential process, where only steps 1 and 4 are obvious to you and sometimes to others. The primary and most important causation mechanisms are going on invisibly inside your brain and body (steps 2 and 3).

Thus, external events NEVER cause you to get angry. They only begin the process that results in you experiencing anger. The true causes are all internal, and they are all invisible as well.

If you've been trying to stop yourself from repeatedly getting angry in response to minor incidents on the road and haven't been able to succeed, you now know the reason.

You've been missing the two most important internal pieces of the anger puzzle.

How Human Brains Work

You, me, and all other drivers on the road today all have human brains. These brains all function based on how they've been **conditioned** to perform. As you go through life, from birth to death, your brain is constantly being reshaped and conditioned. You've also inherited patterns of brain activity that have evolved over millions of years of prior human experience, development, and evolution.

One thing our brains currently do, which they learned to do millions of years ago, is they are **constantly filtering** everything we see and take notice of.

Millions of years ago, life and death threats were present everywhere. Our brains needed the ability to quickly assess a given situation and cause us to take decisive action. Do we run, or do we stay? Are we safe, or is there danger nearby? Is this new person a stranger, friend, or foe?

The problem our brains faced back then, as they do now, is there is just too much data coming into our senses from the external world. If you identified and calculated the total number of discreet data bits impinging on your senses at any point in time, the number would be enormous.

So, our brains needed a solution to this problem. Enter the evolutionary function of **filtering**. Our brains constantly filter everything we see and observe **before we actually perceive it**. In other words, our brains are being highly selective in what they allow us to see.

Our brains NEVER give us a full, truthful, and complete view of the real word.

Our brains are ALWAYS simplifying, condensing, and chunking down what they think is essential or critical for us to pay attention to. *Thus, our brains never allow us to see the world as it actually is or external events as they truthfully occur.*

Instead, we always see an edited, condensed version of the external world, with many things left out and sometimes things added or distorted.

For example, if you were bitten by a dog when you were three, you probably have a "dogs are dangerous" filter in your brain. If you did have such an experience as a child and you encountered a strange dog one day, you would get scared because your brain filter would tell you, "All dogs are dangerous." But if you grew up and didn't have such a formative experience and you encountered a strange dog one day, your brain filter might be, "Oh, what a cute-looking, innocent animal."

When a dog appears in our environment, people with different internal brain filters will have vastly different experiences and emotional reactions from the exact same external trigger.

The Three-Filter Framework for Understanding Human Anger

All human emotions come from a small number of filters that activate inside our brains. *These filters determine how we automatically view and evaluate any situation that renders us emotional.* It turns out there are only three primary filters that give rise to our feelings of anger:

Filter 1: "Someone or something did something bad or wrong that they shouldn't have done."

Filter 2: "Someone or something was hurt, harmed, or negatively impacted by the bad/wrong thing that was done."

Filter 3: "The person or thing who did the bad/wrong behavior was unilaterally (100%) responsible or to blame."

For example, someone cuts you off in traffic and you become angry. Why did you experience this emotional reaction?

Filter 1: Cutting you (or anyone else) off is viewed as "bad" or "wrong."

Filter 2: Your brain tells you that you were negatively impacted—alarmed, put in danger, disrespected, etc.

Filter 3: Your brain tells you that the driver who cut you off was unilaterally responsible or to blame.

Note: You can go back and do the same exercise for all of the other internal causes of anger and road rage identified in the previous chapter. Take a few moments to do this so you can confirm for yourself that they are all variations of these three primary themes or narratives. You'll see they are all variations of:

1. Bad/Wrong
2. Negative Impact
3. Unilateral Blame

For example, if someone driving behind you suddenly accelerates, cuts across the double yellow line, passes you at high speed, and then sharply merges back into the lane ahead of you, and you get angry about this, here's why:

1. You viewed it as "bad/wrong" behavior.
2. You experienced or could have experienced "negative impacts."
3. You saw the other driver as being "unilaterally responsible/to blame."

When you see the world or events through these three specific filters, your brain and body release chemicals that result in the emotion of anger.

Now, if you experienced a different emotional reaction, say anxiety, it would be because a different set of internal filters got activated inside your brain. But whenever you experience anger, we know **with 100% certainty** that your brain made you look through these three primary anger-producing filters described above.

Our brain's filtering process is the second step (which is totally invisible) in the 1-**2**-3-4 anger generation process.

If you've ever seen a Superman movie, TV series, or comic book, you know that Superman has x-ray vision. This ability allows him to see things mortal humans can't normally see. This also gives him a tremendous advantage in certain situations.

Well, guess what? By purchasing this book and reading this chapter, you now have x-ray vision for understanding the invisible internal causes of human anger. You now have that as a superpower which most other people lack.

If you write down the three filters outlined above, and place them on an index card, a sticky note, or on your cell phone or computer, where you can easily refer to them, **you will always be able to see the internal causes of anger** most human beings repeatedly miss. This will now give you a tremendous advantage in freeing yourself from road rage and other forms of unwanted anger in your life.

A New Perspective on Driving

By shifting your focus from external events to internal causes—specifically, the three primary anger-producing brain filters noted above—you can eventually find peace, calm, and control in all of your driving journeys.

Driving will become less about getting from point A to point B as quickly as possible without interruptions and more about navigating challenges with patience, compassion, resilience, and deeper understandings.

CHAPTER 9

Here's the Cure
(WARNING: TOUGH LOVE AHEAD)

Ending road rage is possible for all human beings, regardless of age, but it requires something special. It starts with what you just learned in the previous chapter. But it requires more than simply knowing the invisible internal causes (the three specific filters) generating your angry feelings and subsequent angry behaviors.

By the way, as you saw in the previous chapter, you can summarize these filters with just six words to make them easy to remember:

1. Bad/Wrong

2. Negative Impact

3. Unilateral Blame

In addition to knowing these three filters, curing yourself of anger requires confronting hard truths about yourself, how your brain functions, and more importantly, how your brain often **tricks you** and makes you feel that you are right about your beliefs, opinions, and viewpoints when you may actually be wrong—either partly or completely.

It also requires a little tough love from a mentor like me who has wrestled with these tendencies of our human brains and emerged victorious.

What Is Tough Love?

I'm sure you've heard the term "tough love" before. Maybe you've even experienced it at times during your lifespan.

Tough love isn't about being mean, harsh, or uncaring; it's about caring for someone so much that you're willing to tell them the truth even when it's hard. It's when someone goes way out of their way to help you grow into the best version of yourself, even if it feels uncomfortable for you in the moment.

This chapter is all about giving you the secret of how to cure your road rage and then pushing you with a little tough love, so you will be motivated to embrace it.

What's The Cure?

To be direct, here is the cure for road rage and all other forms of unwanted anger: You've got to develop a counterintuitive mindset.

The Anger Cure Mindset: *Instead of thinking and feeling that you are right and justified whenever you get angry, you need to start assuming that you probably are wrong about one or more of the three primary filters your brain is using to make you angry.*

Note: You won't think you are wrong or feel you are wrong when you consciously choose to adopt this counterintuitive anger-releasing mindset, but once you figure out how your brain has secretly tricked you, you will eventually appreciate that it is the best and most truthful way to look at things.

OK. You may be hating me a little right now. But that's the nature of tough love. This advice—to always assume you are probably wrong about something whenever you get angry—may seem demeaning when you first hear it. But with an open mind and just a little bit of practice, you will eventually realize it is actually true. You'll also discover that embracing it, rather than resisting it, can make your life a whole lot better.

The dirty little secret about anger is that most people (including you) understand it backward. Most people incorrectly believe their anger is caused by rightness or accurate views of the world, when it is secretly and invisibly being caused by wrongness or inaccurate views that your brain is automatically feeding you.

That's why you need a counterintuitive mindset to free yourself.

The little-known truth about anger is that it is often caused by:

- Incorrect viewpoints, not correct or justifiable viewpoints;
- False beliefs, ungrounded opinions, and distorted perceptions, not honest, reasonable judgments and evaluations;
- Our brains secretly playing tricks on us, making it very hard for us to realize that we have indeed been conned.

The bottom line is that anger almost always comes from **wrongness**, not rightness, and this is the **single most important truth** you must grasp about road rage to cure yourself permanently.

Note: *If you want a more detailed explanation of how human anger is almost always caused by wrongness and not rightness, I again refer you to my more complete work on eliminating unwanted anger,* **Dr. Orman's Life Changing Anger Cure,** *published in April, 2024. Here is the link to check it out and purchase it on Amazon:* http://BestAngerBook.com

This chapter offers a no-nonsense approach to overcoming road rage and other forms of unwanted anger. It gives you practical steps and a powerful counterintuitive mindset shift that goes way beyond temporary fixes. For young drivers ready to transform their driving experience and their lives, the cure starts in earnest here.

Here is the Path to Your Road Rage Cure:

Step 1: Stop Blaming Others

The first step in curing road rage is accepting responsibility for your emotions. Blaming other drivers or external circumstances will not lead to personal growth, increased wisdom, or change; it will just lead to more anger.

Acknowledge that your emotional reactions are within your control, even if you don't yet know how to exercise this control, and commit to taking ownership of your emotions and your reactive behaviors.

Note: It should be easier for you to accept full responsibility for your anger now that you have read to this point in the book. If your brain is making you angry, by using the three filters I have described, it's not other people's fault. It may look like it's their fault, but you should have enough awareness and wisdom by now to know that's not the case.

Step 2: Identify Your Usual External Triggers

Some people are more sensitive or reactive to certain triggers than to others. Pay attention to the situations that frequently ignite your anger. Is it being cut off? Slow traffic? Rude gestures?

Note: Please see Appendix A for a helpful list of potential road rage triggers.

By identifying these triggers, you can start anticipating and preparing for them (by telling the truth about them), thereby reducing their emotional impact.

You will still need to do the deeper work of taking on and defeating your internal causes (again, by telling the truth about them), but knowing what is likely to trigger you externally can also be helpful.

Step 3: Challenge Your Automatic Beliefs, Opinions, and Perceptions

Many road rage episodes are fueled by unrealistic beliefs, such as:

- "I must always be in control."
- "Other drivers should always respect me."
- "Being delayed is unacceptable."

- "I can never let anyone cut in front of me."
- "I can't let anyone slow me down."

These are nothing more than examples of your brain tricking you into believing things that aren't true about other drivers or how the world really works.

For example, "I must always be in control" is a foolish goal. There are many things in life you can't control, and when you encounter them, it is best to relax and leave them alone. You can't always control traffic flow or other drivers' behavior, the weather, or the locations of road construction or randomly occurring accidents.

Note: This is just one illustrative example of what it means to "tell yourself the truth" in direct contrast to the anger-producing lies your brain is feeding you. See Appendix B for some other examples.

To assume "other drivers should always respect me" is equally asinine. Some drivers will; some won't. But to expect that everyone should or will respect you is to grossly misunderstand how human beings function.

And the idea in your brain that "being delayed is unacceptable" is another immature and impossible goal to achieve. Everyone gets delayed at times. That's life. Being delayed is neither good nor bad . . . it just is. You can treat it as something bad (and then get angry), or you can treat it as something good or neutral. It's your choice. You are not a victim of being delayed, unless your brain tricks you into believing that you are (which is nonsense).

Note: More truth-telling examples can be found in Appendix B.

If you want to cure yourself of road rage and other forms of unwanted anger, you'll need to assume (counterintuitively) that your brain is probably tricking you or lying to you whenever you become angry. Then, you must start challenging the specific internal beliefs, opinions, and perceptions that emerge from the three anger-producing filters your brain is using to upset you.

Challenge them by asking yourself: Is the first filtered view of reality true? Is it helpful? Is the next filtered view true or helpful? Replacing rigid beliefs and filtered perceptions with more flexible and truthful ones can instantly reduce both anger and frustration.

Step 4: Practice Radical Honesty and Acceptance

Radical honesty and radical acceptance mean acknowledging reality without resistance and without telling lies or other false stories (i.e., telling the truth).

Traffic jams, mistakes by other drivers, and delays are part of driving. Instead of fighting these realities, practice accepting them as neutral or even potentially positive events. One way to view them more positively is to remember that if you are serious about getting rid of your road rage, the more road events that trigger you, the more opportunities you will have to apply the corrective insights and tools you are learning about in this book. This shift in perspective, followed by ongoing practice in making appropriate shifts in your thinking and actions, can drastically reduce your anger.

Step 5: Get An Accountability Partner

Sharing your goal of overcoming road rage with a trusted friend or family member can be highly empowering. Regular check-ins provide encouragement and accountability. Knowing someone is rooting for you can also make it easier to stay on track.

When you are feeling angry and are struggling to see how your brain may be tricking you or sending you false or incomplete narratives, sometimes the insights and perspectives of others can be very helpful.

Remember, it's your own brain that is tricking you, and it is very skilled at concealing what it is doing. This is where the brain of another person can help you identify the falsehoods coming from your own brain more easily.

Step 6: Reflect and Learn

After each drive where anger may have surfaced, take a moment to reflect. How did your internal filters take over your perceptions and your thinking? What were you able to do well? What could you improve? By learning from your experiences, you'll gradually build the self-awareness and skills needed to stay calm and relaxed in future situations.

Tough Love: It's Not About Them—It's About You

This is the hard truth: Road rage isn't about bad drivers, traffic, or delays. **It's about you vs. your own brain.** And your brain is very skilled at keeping you in the dark.

CHAPTER 10

You Are Not as Smart as You Think You Are (Tough Love Part 2)

The problem most drivers who experience road rage have is that they think they are way smarter, better, or more considerate drivers than most other people on the road. This is just another way our brains are constantly tricking us.

One of the most pervasive barriers to ending road rage is **overestimation**—thinking you are more considerate, road-wise, or exceptional behind the wheel. This sense of superiority not only increases frustration when others don't meet your personal standards but also blinds you to your own mistakes and deficiencies. The journey to becoming a calmer, more focused driver begins with **humility**.

The Illusion of Superiority

Studies consistently show that most drivers rate themselves as "above average," which is a mathematical impossibility! This phenomenon, known as the Dunning-Kruger effect, suggests that individuals with limited knowledge or skills often overestimate their abilities. In driving, this manifests as believing other drivers are the problem while your actions are pure, noble, and always justified.

Why Overestimation Fuels Anger

Overestimation creates unrealistic expectations. When you believe you're the smartest, fastest, most caring, or most skilled driver on the road, you expect others to conform to your standards. When they don't, frustration turns to anger. Recognizing this faulty mindset is the first step to defusing it.

The Power of Self-Awareness

Humility isn't about putting yourself down but seeing yourself more clearly. It's about telling the truth and recognizing when your brain is telling you lies, which is more often than we like to admit.

For example, like everyone else, you are human and prone to errors. If your brain tells you otherwise, it's just lying to you.

Understanding your own limitations, particularly by appreciating that all human beings have brains that constantly trick us and lie to us, will make it easier to extend patience and empathy to others.

Practical Steps to Cultivate Humility

1. **Reflect on Mistakes:** After each drive, ask yourself: Did I make any errors myself? Could I have handled the situation better? Did I judge any other driver much too harshly? What might be going on for other drivers who are not meeting my expectations that I didn't consider? Reflecting on your own actions and automatic tendencies builds self-awareness.

2. **Listen to Feedback:** If passengers, family members, or peers point out your problematic driving habits or attitudes, resist the urge to dismiss them. Your brain will want you to think nothing is wrong with your attitudes, driving habits, or other behaviors on the road. Consider that your brain may be tricking you and that others who are close to you can discern the truth about you better than you can. Consider their perspectives and use them to improve (by using their assistance in defeating your brain's trickery and self-deception).

3. **Learn from Others:** Developing humility is a challenge for all of us in life. We live in a society that encourages us to be right and egoistic, and therefore we have brains that make it hard to admit when we are wrong. To combat these strong counterforces in our lives, surround yourself with truth-seekers who regularly debunk generally accepted "truths." Read their books, watch their online videos, go to a few live talks. Learn how they overcome the workings of their own brains and society's false collective assumptions so you can get better at doing this for yourself.

The Role of Cognitive Biases

Cognitive biases, such as the Dunning-Kruger effect, the illusion of control, and confirmation bias, reinforce overconfidence and overestimation. For example, you might attribute a near miss to your quick reflexes (superiority mindset) rather than acknowledging that you were speeding (honesty and humility).

Psychologists and other mental health experts have determined that humans are subject to hundreds of common cognitive biases. This is one more example of how our brains constantly trick us, which is the ultimate source of all unwanted anger and road rage. Challenging these biases helps you see situations more objectively.

Embracing a Growth Mindset

A growth mindset views challenges and mistakes as opportunities to learn. Instead of blaming external factors for a frustrating drive, ask yourself: What can I learn from this, especially what can I learn about myself and how or why my brain reacted as it did? Adopting this mindset transforms every drive into a chance to grow as a driver and a person. Over time, if you do this regularly, your road rage will lessen and eventually disappear.

The Liberation of Letting Go

When you let go of the need to prove your superiority or to believe that your personal judgments of others are always true, driving becomes less stressful. You no longer feel compelled to "teach lessons," "punish offenders," or "win" on the road. Instead, you can focus on what truly matters: perceiving events on the road more honestly, not letting your brain repeatedly trick you, and reaching your destination safely and calmly.

YOU ARE NOT AS SMART AS YOU THINK YOU ARE (TOUGH LOVE PT. 2)

In the next chapter, we'll explore another critical mindset shift: letting go of the need to always be right and learning to approach driving with even more humility and clarity.

"External events NEVER directly cause us to react emotionally, no matter how undesirable they might be."

CHAPTER 11

You Are Not as Right as You Think and Feel You Are (Tough Love Part 3)

Road rage is often fueled by the belief that you are in the right and others are in the wrong. This sense of certainty can make it difficult to see situations objectively, creating a cycle of frustration and anger. This is one of the primary ways your brain keeps tricking you into becoming angry, when anger is neither necessary nor justified. It is the **second invisible cause** of human anger, the third step in the actual 1-2-**3**-4 anger generation process.

In this chapter, we'll explore how letting go of the need to always be right can lead to greater emotional freedom and more peaceful driving experiences.

The Second Invisible Cause of Anger and Road Rage

Earlier in this book, I introduced you to the concept that emotion generation for human beings is not a 1-2 cause/effect process. External events NEVER directly cause us to react emotionally, no matter how undesirable they might be.

Our emotions are always caused by **internal factors** that neither we nor other people typically see. Thankfully, over forty years ago, I discovered that anger generation (and other emotions as well) always emerges from a four-step process: 1-2-3-4, where steps 2 and 3 are invisible internal causes.

In Chapter 8, I showed you that the second step in this process (the first invisible internal cause) is the three specific filters your brain uses to seduce you to look at events in ways that are guaranteed to make you angry:

1. Bad/Wrong
2. Negative Impact
3. Unilateral Blame

Now, I can explain the third step in this four-step model: the second invisible cause is how your brain gets you to automatically think you are right. Not only does your brain give you three specific filters to look through whenever it makes you angry, but immediately after giving you those three filters, **it immediately tells you that all three of them are absolutely true.** This step is also occurring in our brains and is totally invisible as well!

Your brain wants you to believe that everything it is inducing you to see is 100% true, even though the essential nature and purpose of brain filtering is to leave out lots of data (remember, human brains are simplifying filtering machines).

So whenever you are angry, your brain tricked you TWICE! First, it tricked you by giving you filtered infortion and filtered views of reality, which leave out many elements and can even distort the ones you see. And then, it **doubles down** on these filtered "realities" by convincing you that nothing could possibly be wrong with them and that absolutely nothing of importance was distorted or left out.

In other words, with this second diabolical invisible step, your brain essentially tells you, "Hey, I'm your brain. You can trust me. I would never lie to you," as it lies to you again and again and tries to keep you forever in the dark.

The Illusion of Absolute Rightness

When driving, it's easy to think that your perspective is the only valid one (which is what your brain wants you to believe). Whether it's a car merging into your lane directly ahead of you or someone driving too slowly, the assumption is often that they're wrong and you're right. But this black-and-white thinking (which your brain has been conditioned to engage in) ignores the complexities of road situations and human behavior.

The Cost of Being Right

The need to prove you're right comes with significant costs:

1. **Increased Stress:** Constantly judging others and defending your perspectives adds unnecessary tension.
2. **Escalated Conflicts:** Trying to "teach a lesson" or "correct" other drivers often leads to aggressive encounters.

3. **Missed Opportunities for Growth:** By focusing on others' mistakes, you miss the chance to improve your own self-awareness, your own truth-telling skills, and your own driving and emotion-processing habits.
4. **Possible Loss of License or Jail Time.**
5. **Sometimes Even Death.**

Questioning Your Assumptions

To break free from this very common anger-generating mindset, start by questioning your assumptions instead of always believing they are true. Ask yourself:

- Is it possible that the other driver made an honest mistake?
- Could the other driver be experiencing a real problem, like a screaming child, a heart attack, engine trouble, or other interruptions?
- Could there be factors influencing their driving behavior that I'm unaware of?
- How might my own biases be shaping my interpretation of the situation?

The Power of Empathy

Empathy is a powerful antidote to the need to be right. Instead of viewing other drivers as adversaries or wrongdoers, try to understand their perspective. Maybe they're new to the area, dealing with an emergency, or simply having a bad day. Shifting your focus from judgment to compassion and understanding can diffuse anger and create a sense of connection.

Strategies for Letting Go of Rightness

1. **Practice Mindful Observation:** Notice your thoughts when you feel wronged on the road. Acknowledge them without judgment and let them pass. The problems (and anger) come when you take them too seriously.

2. **Reframe the Situation:** Instead of labeling a driver's actions as "wrong," describe them neutrally: "That car merged into my lane unexpectedly."

3. **Focus on What You Can Control:** Accept that you can't change other drivers' behavior but can choose how you respond.

The Freedom of Letting Go

Letting go of the need to be right isn't about condoning bad behavior—it's about freeing yourself from unnecessary anger and frustration. When you release this burden, driving becomes less about competition and more about cooperation. You'll find it easier to stay calm, even in challenging situations.

"Knowing when your brain is lying to you, which turns out to be 98% of the time whenever you get angry, is one of the keys to eliminating road rage or any other type of anger."

CHAPTER 12

Three Ways Your Brain Is Tricking You When You Get Angry

If you think it's bad that your brain tricks you TWICE whenever you get angry (or have any other strong negative emotion), it's actually worse.

Your brain tricks you in **three ways** whenever you get angry.

Note: Obviously, your brain isn't always tricking you or lying to you whenever you have a strong emotion like fear, or anger, or guilt. SOMETIMES your brain is telling you the truth, but much of the time it is mostly lying. Knowing when your brain is lying to you, which turns out to be 98% of the time whenever you get angry, is one of the keys to eliminating road rage or any other type of anger. In other words, assume your brain is tricking you, probably in multiple ways, and then go find out how this is true and then overcome the trickery (by reminding yourself what is really true).

The Third Way Your Brain Tricks You When You Are Angry

The first way your brain tricks you when you get angry is by giving you filtered, incomplete, and often untrue lity. Once again, for the emotion of anger these perspectives are:

1. Bad/Wrong
2. Negative Impact
3. Unilateral Blame

These "internal realities" are often incomplete, misleading, and possibly even wrong.

Note: Sometimes when you are angry only one of these filtered "internal realities" will be false, and the other two might be true. Other times it may be two that are false. And sometimes all three will be defective. However, it only takes debunking one of the three "internal realities" to bust up the emotion and have it instantly lose its power and control over you.

Next, after giving you these filtered realities, your brain immediately convinces you they are all true and complete—nothing is wrong, nothing is left out. This is pure second-level trickery, since we know that the filtering process that our brain is using ALWAYS LEAVES THINGS OUT and very often gets things wrong.

Now, that's terrible to get double-tricked and double-hoodwinked into becoming angry by your own brain! And even worse that the trickery keeps happening over and over again, until you wake up from your deep sleep and recognize that it's going on.

The solution to this common human dilemma, at this point, would be very straightforward—recognize that whenever you are angry your brain is double-tricking you, and

THREE WAYS YOUR BRAIN IS TRICKING YOU WHEN YOU GET ANGRY

then do something to ferret out the key lies and distortions that are actually making you angry.

Not so fast!

Your brain is not going to let you take control away from it so easily. It has one more dirty trick in its bag. And it's a sinister one at that.

After tricking you twice to get you angry, your brain now uses a third slight-of-hand maneuver—**it uses the emotion of anger** it just caused you to experience (through the initial double-trickery) to trick you a third time. Your brain uses the FEELING OF ANGER to cloak and protect its original double-trickery.

It doesn't want you to question the truthfulness of the three anger filters it gave you, one or more of which are usually not true. To get you off track, it teaches you to believe that whenever you are angry, THE FEELING OF ANGER MEANS THAT YOU ARE RIGHT!!!

You've heard of "righteous anger" before, haven't you?

The term **"righteous anger"** typically refers to a strong feeling of indignation or moral outrage that arises in response to perceived injustice, wrongdoing, or evil. Righteous anger is often seen as motivated by a desire to uphold ethical principles or defend others (or yourself) who are being wronged.

Key Characteristics of Righteous Anger:

1. **Moral Foundation:** It is rooted in a sense of justice or moral values rather than self-interest.

2. **Focused on Change:** The goal of righteous anger is often to address or correct a wrong, rather than merely to express frustration or hostility.

3. **Empathy-Driven:** It may arise from compassion or concern for others, especially when they are victims of injustice or harm.

4. **Purposeful Action:** It often motivates constructive actions, such as advocating for justice, standing up for the oppressed, standing up for yourself, or challenging unethical behavior.

Examples of Righteous Anger:

- Advocating for social justice or human rights when faced with systemic inequality or oppression.
- Speaking out against abuse, corruption, or exploitation.
- Defending someone who is being unfairly treated or harmed.
- Maintaining proper driving decorum on the roadways for all.

The key point about righteous anger is contained in the term "righteous"—**it makes you feel right**. And this is true of all forms of anger.

Your brain wants you to believe that if you have strong feelings of anger, **you must be right and justified about the way you are looking at the world.**

THREE WAYS YOUR BRAIN IS TRICKING YOU WHEN YOU GET ANGRY

- You must be right about what your internal filters (i.e., your brain) is telling you to believe.
- You must be right that someone or something did a bad or wrong or unjust thing.
- You must be right that someone or something was hurt, harmed, or negatively impacted.
- And you must be right that the offending person or thing was unilaterally responsible or 100% to blame for their behavior and any negative impacts that resulted.

Note: If you get angry at your computer, your car, or your lawnmower, your brain is telling you: that "thing" did something bad/wrong, that "thing" caused negative impacts, and that "thing" was unilaterally responsible or to blame.

Your brain wants you to believe that if you feel angry, your feelings are "proof" that you are right about what the three filters are telling you to see and believe.

But it's a scam—an ingenious triple-layered scam.

Your brain has cleverly and secretly designed a self-protecting anger-generating system. By first giving you flawed, incomplete viewpoints and then convincing you they are absolutely true, your brain has a system for easily and repeatedly making you angry.

Then, it fortifies and protects this faulty system, by teaching you to believe that whenever you feel angry you must be right!

Well, if you feel right, are you going to investigate and deeply probe for how your brain might be making you wrong? No, that's the last thing you would normally do. And that's just how your brain wants it.

Checkmate!!!

You were not only tricked twice in order to make you angry. But you were tricked a third time to keep you from exploring how your brain tricked you the first two times. **It's an incredibly ingenious and insidious self-protecting system.** And this is why most people find it very hard to stop getting angry or to correctly understand what's really going on when they get triggered to become emotional.

It's as if their brain functions like the Romulans in *Star Trek*, activating powerful cloaking devices to prevent anyone from attacking their spacecraft.

In this case, **it's the FEELING OF ANGER that becomes the cloaking device**. It makes you feel right, so why would you ever question the validity of the three anger-producing viewpoints your brain has just served up for you?

You've got to wake up and deeply understand this: Your brain doesn't want you to question the three filters.

It wants you to assume they are all true, even when one or more of them may definitely be wrong.

So your brain is not only a simplifying machine, **it's a machine for making you feel right even when you may be wrong.**

In order to end your habitual road rage, or any other habitual form of unwanted anger, you are going to have to understand the game your brain is playing.

THREE WAYS YOUR BRAIN IS TRICKING YOU WHEN YOU GET ANGRY

Your brain is playing 3-D chess.

You, on the other hand, are still playing 2-D checkers. That's why when it comes to understanding and dealing with anger, you keep getting your ass handed to you by your brain, every single time.

It's time to wise up. Your brain is making you angry, and keeping you angry, and you don't have to let this continue. Once you understand what's really going on, you can start learning how to play 3-D chess against your brain and eventually defeat it.

The Media Knows Exactly How Our Brains Work

Have you ever noticed that the media is very good at making us angry, anytime they want? It's their business model, because anger and other strong emotions drive viewership and hence media revenue.

Exactly how does the media make you angry? It feeds you the same three narratives that your brain feeds you to make you angry:

1. Somebody or something did something bad or wrong that they shouldn't have done.
2. Somebody or something was hurt, harmed, or negatively impacted.
3. The person or thing who did the bad/wrong behavior was 100% responsible or to blame.

So, don't take my word for it that this is how your brain creates anger for you. Pay attention to what the real experts at generating anger know and what they do to make you angry. It's the exact same anger-generating process I have described in this book and that your brain uses internally.

And just like your own brain, the media doesn't want you to know how often they are lying to you and how they use tricks and deception to keep you from figuring out how they can so easily and regularly bamboozle you.

CHAPTER 13

A Window Into the Truth About Anger

Windows are a big part of any driving experience. Whether you're behind the wheel of a car, truck, bus, or any other vehicle, you're usually surrounded by glass—windshields, side windows, rear windows—all there to protect you from the elements and help you monitor the world around you. We tend to take these windows for granted, rarely thinking about them beyond keeping them clean and clear.

But imagine there was another kind of window—a window that lets you see straight into the heart of human anger. A window that lets you see the deeper truth about anger in general, and road rage in particular. Guess what? You already have it. And you don't need fancy equipment or anything else to use it or keep it clean. It's simply **other drivers' anger at you!**

The Window of Other Drivers' Anger

We've all been there: another driver honks, screams, flips you off, or in some other way makes it crystal clear they're mad at you. In that moment your heart rate spikes and your own temper flares. But now that you've read this book, you know exactly what is fueling their outrage, deep within their brain. Their brain is using the same three filters your brain uses when you get triggered to become angry. This means:

1. **They believe you did something bad or wrong.**
2. **They believe you caused (or almost caused) a negative impact on them or someone/something they care about.**
3. **They believe YOU are 100% at fault or to blame.**

These are the three invisible, internal brain filters through which all human anger emerges.

Unfortunately, most of us respond to someone else's road rage with anger of our own. That's how minor incidents spiral into full-blown road rage, sometimes with tragic outcomes.

But what if someone else getting angry with you on the road is actually a secret opportunity? What if it's a chance to look behind the curtain of human anger? **What if you could use their anger to understand—and ultimately cure—your own?**

The Three Filters We All Share

When another driver accuses you of wrongdoing on the road, they're seeing you through the **very same three filters** that create your own anger and that shape every flare-up of road rage. And while it might feel personal and unfair, it also offers a fascinating insight:

- **They are human, just like you.**
- **They're using the same brain wiring and the same flawed perceptions of "wrongdoing" and "fault" and "shoulds."**
- **When people get angry, they genuinely believe they've been wronged, even if that belief is filled with errors or false assumptions.**

In other words, **it's the exact same process that happens in your head** when you're the one raging.

The difference is that seeing it from the outside (your perspective) can teach you a lot about what's going on inside (their usually flawed perspective).

This is because it's easier to see the truth about human anger when you are the one receiving it rather than dishing it out.

An Unexpected Gift

Before reading this book, you probably saw nothing good about when other drivers aim their anger at you. But once you understand the three-filter model, those infuriating encounters can transform into powerful learning moments.

Why? Because when you're on the receiving end, **you can instantly recognize when someone's anger is based on faulty assumptions:**

- They may have judged you too harshly.
- They might be ignoring their own share of responsibility.
- They're likely blowing a small mistake out of proportion.

You can instantly sense that their angry perceptions of you are false, distorted, or wildly exaggerated. **You know the truth about yourself and your motives**, and you can determine quickly that their brain filters are blocking this important information from them.

That clarity is exactly what's missing when **you** are the one in the hot seat, drowning in your own adrenaline and anger. When you're upset, it's much tougher to see the holes in your logic or the exaggerations in your own mind. You feel justified in the moment.

Yet, when someone else is raging at you for an honest mistake—or for something that isn't even your fault—you can see immediately where they're off base.

This "window" into the truth about human anger reveals how anger often stems from inflated expectations, half-truths, and sometimes downright lies. And that's the hidden gift: **once you see how flawed other people's anger at you usually is, you realize your own anger is often just as flawed.**

Anger Through a Flawed Lens

Even in situations where someone's mistake truly hurts you —like if they rear-end your car because they were texting— your anger can feel totally justified. But ask yourself:

- **Is it reasonable to expect other drivers to be 100% perfect all the time?**
- **Haven't you ever made a careless mistake yourself, even if it didn't cause a crash?**

When we're seething with rage, our brains ignore these inconvenient truths. We think, "They should have been paying attention!" even though we know we've all been guilty of daydreaming or glancing at our phones. If we step back and see anger for what it is—**a raw emotional reaction often fueled by unrealistic expectations or other brain filter distortions**—we can start responding differently.

Learning From Other People's Rage

So how do we use this "window" to our advantage?

1. **Acknowledge the Three Filters:** When another driver is angry at you, recognize that they're looking at you through those same internal filters:

    a. They think you did something wrong.

    b. They feel that you've harmed or could have harmed them.

    c. They believe it's entirely your fault.

2. **Spot the Flaws:** Notice immediately if and where their assumptions are off. Are they blaming you for a shared mistake? Are they overreacting to something minor?

3. **Reflect on Your Own Patterns:** Ask yourself, "When I get angry at other drivers, am I falling into the same mental traps?" If it's easy for you to see the errors in their anger, you can bet there are errors in yours, too.

4. **Stay Calm:** Understanding that anger often arises from faulty filters makes it easier to remain calm.

Instead of letting your temper explode, remind yourself that they're human and that their anger is fueled by misconceptions—just like yours typically is.

5. **Use the Window to Look Inward:** Remember, this window isn't just for observing others; it helps you see your own potential for overreaction. The more you learn from other people's rage, the better you'll get at spotting the same distorted thinking in yourself.

A Window That Looks Both Ways

Your car windows let you look out at the road, but this new window—the one letting you see the truth about anger—does something even more powerful. It points inward, helping you understand your own emotional assumptions, judgments, and flawed expectations. Recognizing that other people's anger can be based on pure misinformation or unrealistic demands reveals that yours often is, too.

And that's the ultimate irony: the next time someone flips you off or lays on the horn, they will unknowingly be helping you to gain more clarity and control over your own temper, even though they might be losing theirs. **In that moment, you'll realize their emotional meltdown could be your anger breakthrough.**

Embrace this new perspective as you keep driving through life. Appreciate this new window, and watch how your own road rage gradually fades into the rearview mirror.

CHAPTER 14

Inner Peace Through Humility, Honesty, and Clarity

The road to becoming a calmer driver mirrors the journey to personal growth. At its heart, it requires **humility** to acknowledge our flaws and how often our brains trick us and lie to us, **honesty** to face deep truths, and **clarity** to understand the bigger picture. In this chapter, we'll explore how these three qualities can transform your driving and your entire outlook on life.

The Role of Humility

Humility is about recognizing that you don't have all the answers and that, as a human being, you will be wrong frequently, including many times when you feel certain you are right. With regard to road rage, humility is the understanding that every driver, including yourself, is human and prone to mistakes. Embracing humility can:

- **Reduce Ego-Driven Conflicts:** Let go of the need to "win" or dominate on the road.
- **Foster Empathy:** Understand that others may be facing challenges you can't see or sometimes even imagine.

- **Encourage Learning:** Use each drive and each emotional reaction as an opportunity to learn and improve.

Honesty: Facing Deeper Truths

True change begins with honesty. Acknowledge your triggers, patterns, and the role YOU play in creating road rage scenarios. Ask yourself:

- What drives my anger? (Answer: it's the three filters.)
- Are my reactions appropriate to the situation? (Usually not.)
- How can I take responsibility for my behavior? (Stop blaming and criticizing others and start telling the truth about what your own brain is doing.)

Honesty isn't about self-blame; it's about self-awareness and knowing how your brain tricks you (in all three ways) whenever you are angry. By facing these deeper truths and looking beyond what your brain is telling you to believe, you can start to address the previously invisible root causes of your emotional reactions.

Clarity: Seeing the Bigger Picture

Clarity allows you to step back and view situations from a broader, more complete, and more truthful perspective. Instead of fixating on minor annoyances and seeing them as bigger infractions than they truly are, focus instead on what truly matters:

- **Your Safety:** Avoiding aggressive behaviors reduces the risk of accidents.
- **Your Health:** Staying calm protects your physical and mental well-being.
- **Your Relationships:** Modeling compassion and composure can inspire others to do the same. Repeatedly getting angry is a turn-off that can damage relationships you care about.
- **Your Quality of Life:** Your brain doesn't only trick you when it comes to producing anger. It tricks you in many other ways in your life. When you learn to take control of your anger and eliminate it by recognizing and defeating the invisible tactics your brain is using against you, you will strengthen your ability to defeat your brain when it's causing other mischief in your life. And trust me, if left unchecked, your brain will produce a lot of mischief, problems, and unnecessary stress.

Practical Steps to Achieve Inner Peace

1. **Daily Reflection:** Take a few minutes each day to review your actions and thoughts, especially regarding your efforts to reduce or eliminate angry reactions. Celebrate your progress and identify areas for continued growth.

2. **Practice, Practice, Practice:** From now on, every time you get angry in any situation, not just on the road, refer to your list of three anger-producing filters and

confirm that your brain has indeed induced you to look at what happened through these three automatic perspectives. If you are angry, the three filters MUST HAVE BEEN ACTIVATED WITHIN YOU. The more you practice recognizing this is true, the better and quicker you will become at identifying the internal causes of your angry reactions over time.

3. **Set Intentions:** Before each drive, set a positive intention, such as "I will remain patient and focused," "If I get angry, I will shift from blaming others to looking within myself," or "If I get angry, I will try to look at the situation differently than my brain is directing me to view it."

The Ripple Effect of Change

When you cultivate these practices of greater self-awareness and telling the truth about what is happening, you will increase your inner peace and significantly reduce your anger. This extends far beyond the driver's seat.

As you become more relaxed and less reactive behind the wheel, your calmness influences passengers, other drivers, and even your loved ones. By choosing humility, honesty, and clarity, you create a ripple effect that inspires others to do the same.

A Lifelong Journey

The principles revealed in this book for curing road rage and eliminating other forms of unwanted anger are not a quick fix but a lifelong journey. Each drive is an opportunity to practice, learn, and grow from what you have learned here. Committing to this path can transform road rage into resilience, frustration into focus, and anger into deeper self-awareness.

As we approach the end of this book, remember that the road to calmness, inner peace, greater clarity, and a life free of unwanted anger begins from within. Your mission, should you choose to accept it, is to drive safely, live peacefully, grant compassion and forgiveness to fellow drivers, and inspire others to do the same.

Your mission is also to remember and then investigate the three filters, each and every time you get triggered to become angry.

"Your brain wants you to keep thinking you are right, especially when it has gone to great lengths to make you angry."

CHAPTER 15

Putting It All Together: Implementing the Cure

You have now reached the point in this book where I can show you exactly how to implement the Road Rage Cure and the overall Anger Cure for any anger in your life.

You now have a new foundation of understanding, based on the following key principles:

a) Your brain is a simplifying, filtering machine.

b) Your brain is constantly lying to you and deceiving you ... because it is a simplifying, filtering machine.

c) External events do not cause your emotions (these are just triggers that begin the emotion-generation process).

d) Invisible, internal filters in your brain cause your emotions to arise.

e) You, and other people, cannot see these invisible, internal causes of your emotions.

f) But you can become aware of them by reading a book like this.

g) The primary internal causes of your emotions are a small group of specific filters (thought patterns, beliefs, perception habits) that your brain activates to create "internal realities" which are the actual causes of your emotions but which are often partly or completely false.

h) For anger, three specific brain filters cause this emotion (in all human beings) regardless of the triggering event.

i) For anger, these three internal brain filters are: 1) Bad/Wrong, 2) Negative Impact, and 3) Unilateral Blame.

j) Immediately after giving you these three filtered "realities," your brain lies to you and tells you they are all correct, even though one or more are usually not completely true.

k) The combination of your brain automatically making you look at events through the three anger-producing filters, coupled with your brain convincing you all three "internal realities" are absolutely true, is what constitutes the internal mechanism that generates your internal emotion of anger (these are the invisible steps 2 and 3 in the 1-**2**-**3**-4 anger-generation model, where 1 represents the triggering event and 4 represents the anger you feel).

l) The same process is how all of our human emotions get created, both positive ones and negative ones—the only difference is that the originating brain filters are different for each distinct emotion.

m) Once you feel an emotion, your brain goes into action and lies to you again, making you think that if you feel so strongly about something, your viewpoints (internal filtered "realities") that generated the emotion must be true and accurate . . . even when they are not.

n) If you want to free yourself from road rage or any other type of anger, your job is to understand these points above . . . and then defend yourself appropriately.

o) Your job is to understand what your brain is doing to you EVERY TIME you become emotional and then learn how to defeat your brain and the games/deceptions it is running on you.

Here is How You Do This:

First, notice when you've been triggered to become emotional.

Second, correctly identify the specific emotion or emotions you are experiencing (sometimes it can be a series of emotions in rapid succession—for example you blow up after getting angry, then feel guilty for having done so, then you feel ashamed and embarrassed, all within seconds).

Third, if you are angry about anything, large or small, know that the three anger-producing filters MUST HAVE BEEN ACTIVATED in your brain. This will be the case 100% of the time, whether you believe it or not!

Fourth, SUSPECT that one or more of your internal filtered "realities" will be distorted, partially incorrect, totally incorrect, missing critical data, philosophically naïve, or otherwise inaccurate.

Fifth, look at your list of anger-producing filters that you previously wrote down (use your anger index card or other notation system to make this easy) and know that this is how you MUST BE LOOKING AT THINGS/THINKING ABOUT THINGS in order to feel angry.

Sixth, start questioning and challenging each of these three "internal realities" until you find one or more that isn't wholly true.

Seventh, discover or remind yourself about what is actually true and different from the "reality" your brain wants you to believe.

Eighth, once you successfully "un-trick" yourself, your anger will lessen or completely disappear.

Ninth, once gone, your anger could reappear quickly because your brain likes sending you false "realities" over and over.

Tenth, no problem here—just repeat the seventh step above (reminding yourself what is true), which should be easier now that you've done the work to execute this step the first time (Seventh Step).

Eleventh, repeat the tenth step/seventh step (reminding yourself what is true) as many times as you need to combat your brain's tendency to repeatedly trick you by sending you false "internal realities" over and over again.

Home Free

You now have a reliable and repeatable "system" for freeing yourself of unwanted anger anytime you choose.

You can use this system to deal with any road rage triggered by any external event, such as traffic jams, "inconsiderate" drivers, inattentive drivers, motorcyclists, bikers, pedestrians, road-blocking protesters, inexperienced drivers, elderly drivers, truck drivers, construction delays, weather conditions, etc.

You can also use it to deal with anger at work, anger with your spouse, anger with your kids, anger at strangers on a bus, anger at the government, anger at politicians, anger at "climate deniers" or "climate alarmists," anger at slow-moving cashier lines in stores, etc.

This system WORKS every time you use it, provided you use it correctly (as outlined above) and that you do the hard work of fighting to tell the truth.

Remember, your brain is very skilled at keeping you from knowing what's true. It's been secretly doing this to humans for millions of years.

Most people never wake up to how deceiving their own brains can be. That's why most people don't figure out how to cure themselves of road rage or any other form of unwanted anger, even though we all have the innate ability to do this.

You, however, are now awake, alert, and well-equipped to take on and defeat your road rage. You now have the knowledge and anger-busting system to do so.

The only things now that might get in your way are your pride, stubbornness, and desire to keep thinking you are right when you are often wrong.

Your brain wants you to keep thinking you are right, especially when it has gone to great lengths to make you angry. That's how your brain keeps winning the anger game and why you end up repeatedly as the loser.

The people who wake up and start taking control of their anger do so by first realizing that whenever they are triggered to feel angry . . . THEY ARE PROBABLY SEEING THINGS WRONGLY OR THINKING ABOUT THINGS WRONGLY . . . even if they believe they are not.

Convincing you to NOT see this and NOT understand this is how your brain keeps winning. But it's too late for your brain now. By reading this book, you now understand what is really going on inside your head. And now, it's your turn to start winning the anger game.

It's now time for you to step up to the plate and take a few swings for as long as it takes to become a world-class, accomplished hitter.

Your brain doesn't stand a chance . . . once you know how to play the game and you finally know how to win it!

CHAPTER 16
Summary, Conclusions and Next Steps

Road rage is more than an inconvenience; it's a pervasive issue that impacts personal well-being, relationships, and society. This book explores the underlying causes, common misconceptions, and practical solutions to transform the way we drive, perceive, react, and live.

Key Takeaways:

1. **Understanding Young Drivers:** Young drivers face unique challenges due to their developmental stage, societal pressures, and emotional tendencies. Recognizing these factors is crucial to addressing road rage in this age group.

2. **Identifying the True Causes:** Road rage stems not from external triggers but from internal filters that your brain uses to make you angry. Recognizing and then addressing these invisible, internal root causes is the key to lasting change and the cure for this problem, which, until now, has been difficult to overcome.

3. **The Power of Mindset Shifts:** Letting go of overconfidence, the need to be right, and unrealistic

expectations, creates space for empathy, patience, greater self-awareness, calmness, and resilience.

4. **Practical Strategies for Change:** The insights and tools in this book can empower you to eliminate your angry reactions and stay calm, focused, and in control behind the wheel.

5. **The Ripple Effect:** Cultivating calmness and lack of anger on the road extends to other areas of life, improving relationships, health, and overall happiness.

Moving Forward:

Change is not instantaneous, but it is possible. By embracing humility, honesty, and clarity, you can turn each drive into an opportunity for growth and peace. The road to calm driving is the road to a better life—one choice at a time.

As you apply the powerful life lessons from this book, remember: the goal is not perfection but progress. Every moment of calmness you achieve contributes to a safer, more harmonious world for everyone. And after a while, it becomes a new habit that is easier to maintain.

As a young or beginning driver, you actually have much more to gain than older, more experienced drivers who struggle with road rage. By learning how to understand and eliminate most of your anger now, you won't have to suffer the many adverse consequences we older drivers experienced before we woke up.

By learning how to lessen your anger and angry reactions now, you'll have better health, safer travels, better sleep, better interpersonal relationships, more emotionally healthy kids, and many more peaceful, anger-free drives.

Remember, if you are under age 25, your brain and frontal cortex (higher thinking and reasoning functions) are still developing. So the more you practice "outthinking" and "outreasoning" your own brain, the more you strengthen this important seat of wisdom and reasoning.

Note: This type of mental practice is also beneficial to your prefrontal cortex if you are 25 or older.

Thank You and Best Wishes

Thank you for embarking on this transformative journey. Drive safely, live well, and use the lessons in this book to see yourself, your emotions, and other drivers more clearly and truthfully.

Epilogue

I have endeavored, as best as possible, to give you the best guidance, training, and strategies I know of to help you eliminate any road rage problems or other anger problems you might want to get rid of.

I sincerely hope you take the time to practice with the strategies and new perspectives on anger I have laid out for you here. While the system and rationale for arguing with your own brain, whenever it is making you angry, is sound and has proven to be effective by over 40 years of personal and professional experience, it is not always easy to integrate this approach in the beginning.

You could experience dramatic results immediately. But for many, it will take time and repeated experimentation. If you would like my help in implementing this anger elimination approach, I would be happy to discuss personal coaching with you. You can reach me by email at doc@docorman.com.

Also, if you want additional training on how I developed and use this anger elimination method in my own life and in my work with other people, I highly recommend my more extensive book on anger, **Dr. Orman's Life Changing Anger Cure**, which you can check out in this page at Amazon: http://BestAngerBook.com

You can also find other resources for emotions mastery, relationships mastery, and stress mastery at my website http://DocOrman.com

Finally, if you like this approach and think you would enjoy learning about the internal causes of guilt, frustration, fear/anxiety, worry, and sadness, and how to master these five other common emotions, I have a short video training course called **Quick Emotions Mastery (QEM)** that you can complete online, at your own pace, in under four hours. To learn more about this course and purchase it if you wish, go to: http://quickemotionsmastery.com

Appendix A: Common Road Rage Triggers

Below is a list of potential triggers for road rage, organized by categories. These range from minor annoyances to major provocations.

Car Driver–Related

1. **Tailgating** or following too closely.
2. **Cutting off** other drivers without using turn signals.
3. **Driving too slowly** in the fast lane or elsewhere, causing backups.
4. **Sudden braking** or "brake-checking" to intimidate someone behind.
5. Failing to **yield the right-of-way** when merging.
6. **Aggressive weaving** between lanes at high speed.
7. **Blocking intersections** or stoplights by inching forward improperly.
8. **Overly loud music** or honking excessively.
9. **Gestures or other expressions** made by other drivers displeased with you.

Truck Driver–Related

1. Large **blind spots** causing near-collisions or "close calls."
2. **Slow uphill passing**, causing long lines of traffic.
3. **Debris or cargo** blowing off open truck beds.

4. **Aggressive merging** from on-ramps without speed adjustment.
5. **Extended idling** in busy lanes, blocking traffic flow.
6. **Delivery drivers** parking in traffic lanes, blocking traffic flow.

Bus Driver-Related
1. **Frequent, sudden stops** to pick up passengers without clear signals.
2. **Taking up multiple lanes** in tight city streets.
3. **Blocking intersections** while loading or unloading.
4. Abrupt **lane changes** to adhere to a tight schedule.
5. **Heavy exhaust fumes** irritating drivers behind.

Motorcyclists
1. **Lane splitting** or weaving through traffic at high speeds.
2. **Excessive revving** or loud exhaust near other vehicles.
3. **Riding on the shoulder** to bypass heavy traffic.
4. **Unexpected swerving** around cars without signaling.
5. **Speeding in blind spots**, making them difficult to see.

Bicyclists
1. **Riding in the middle of the lane** on busy roads.
2. **Ignoring stop signs** or red lights.
3. **Sudden swerving** into traffic to avoid obstacles.
4. **No lights or reflectors** at night, limiting visibility.
5. **Switching between sidewalk and road** unpredictably.

APPENDIX A: COMMON ROAD RAGE TRIGGERS

Pedestrians
1. **Jaywalking** or crossing mid-block without warning.
2. **Distracted walking** (texting, headphones) leading to unexpected moves.
3. Stepping off the curb **directly into traffic**.
4. **Crossing against the signal** at busy intersections.
5. **Loitering** in crosswalks, slowing or blocking turning vehicles.

Scooters
1. **Riding in car lanes at slow speeds**, creating a speed mismatch.
2. **Abruptly switching** from sidewalk to street.
3. Leaving scooters **parked improperly** in traffic lanes or on sidewalks.
4. **Sudden stops** or sharp turns without signaling.
5. **No helmets** or protective gear, sparking anxiety for other drivers.

Golf Carts
1. **Operating on roads** not meant for golf carts.
2. **Driving significantly below speed limits**, causing long backups.
3. Making **wide turns** or abrupt stops in traffic.
4. Occupants **behaving casually or distracting** the driver.
5. **Poor lighting** or signals, especially at dusk or night.

Runners

1. Running **close to traffic** without reflective clothing or gear.
2. **Darting across streets** to maintain pace without checking traffic.
3. **Ignoring crosswalks** and signals during a run.
4. Jogging on **roads with no sidewalks**, forcing cars to swerve.
5. Wearing **headphones** that block out oncoming vehicle noises.

Pets

1. **Unsecured pets** inside the vehicle, distracting the driver.
2. Dogs **jumping around** in the back seat or open truck bed.
3. **Sudden stops** to avoid hitting animals crossing the road.
4. **Swerving** to avoid stray animals, startling other drivers.
5. Pets **obstructing mirrors or windows** (e.g., a dog with its head out).

Weather

1. **Heavy rain** causing hydroplaning and reduced visibility.
2. **Snow or ice** creating slippery surfaces and slow traffic.
3. **Thick fog** making it hard to see other vehicles or lanes.
4. **High winds** blowing cars or trucks out of their lanes.
5. **Sudden storms** causing panic or unexpected lane changes.

APPENDIX A: COMMON ROAD RAGE TRIGGERS

Construction

1. **Lane closures** or forced merges slowing traffic significantly.
2. **Poorly marked detours** leading to confusion.
3. **Slow-moving construction vehicles** merging into live traffic.
4. **Rough or uneven pavement** causing erratic driving or tire damage.
5. **Noise or bright lights** at night, distracting or startling drivers.

Accidents

1. **Gawking or rubbernecking**, creating unnecessary slowdowns.
2. **Blocked lanes** for emergency responders.
3. **Debris from crashes** scattered on the roadway.
4. **Sudden stops** when drivers see hazard lights ahead.
5. **Stalled vehicles** in traffic lanes, forcing abrupt merges.

Emergency Vehicles

1. **Ambulances, fire trucks, police cars** needing priority and forcing sudden lane changes.
2. **Sirens** startling drivers, causing abrupt braking or swerving.
3. **Drivers not yielding** properly to emergency vehicles.
4. **Blocked intersections** or confusion about right-of-way when multiple emergency vehicles converge.

Rideshare & Taxi Drivers

1. **Stopping suddenly** to pick up or drop off passengers in traffic lanes.
2. **Frequent U-turns** or unexpected detours to follow navigation apps.
3. **Distracted driving** as they manage passenger requests or phone-based app alerts.
4. **Double parking** or obstructing bike lanes/bus lanes while waiting for riders.

Road Infrastructure Issues

1. **Potholes** or poorly maintained roads causing sudden swerves or lane changes.
2. **Poor signage** or faded lane markings leading to confusion and last-minute decisions.
3. **Unclear speed limit changes** (e.g., dropping from 55 mph to 35 mph abruptly).
4. **Malfunctioning traffic lights** causing gridlock or risky intersections.

Tolls and Checkpoints

1. **Long lines** at toll booths, creating impatience.
2. **Drivers searching for change** or an EZ-Pass, holding up traffic.
3. **Confusion over correct lanes** for cash or electronic tolls.
4. **Sudden lane changes** to avoid toll booths or short queues.

APPENDIX A: COMMON ROAD RAGE TRIGGERS

Special Events or Road Closures

1. **Parades, marathons, festivals** causing unexpected detours.
2. **Sports events** leading to heavy congestion near stadiums.
3. **Long waits** and restricted access frustrating already stressed drivers.
4. **Confusing temporary signage** or reroutes that drivers fail to follow correctly.

Whether it's a minor irritation or a major provocation, being aware of what sets you off can help you develop coping strategies and stay calm on the road.

As mentioned in Chapter 9, by identifying these triggers, you can start anticipating and preparing for them (by telling the truth about them), thereby reducing their emotional impact.

You will still need to do the deeper work of taking on and defeating your internal causes (again, by telling the truth about each of the three anger-producing brain filters), but knowing what is likely to trigger you externally can also be helpful.

Appendix B: Examples of Telling the Truth

Following are just a few examples of how to have an honest discussion with your brain whenever it is making you angry. This requires you to tell the truth about any anger-provoking situation, including all of the road rage triggers listed in Appendix A, and then tell the truth about the three anger-producing filters your brain is using.

Note: often multiple things or perspectives can be true or "true-ish" at the same time. For example, it may be true that another driver was speeding and weaving through traffic putting others in potential danger. But it's also true that people sometimes do stupid or dangerous things, that you're probably not going to stop this, that it is foolish to EXPECT others to NEVER do this, and that it makes no sense to get worked up about it when you could easily just stay out of the way and let the emotion go. Also, you could record the incident or get the license plate number and report the dangerous driver. And there are probably several other "truths" that could be discerned from this situation as well.

APPENDIX B: EXAMPLES OF TELLING THE TRUTH

External Trigger	Your Brain Says "True"	What Is/ May Be True
Tailgating too closely	Bad/Wrong	True if too close, but who defines "too close," and can it vary for different people?"
Tailgating too closely	Negative Impact	Yes, you may become scared or worried, but were you actually harmed? Would everyone react with the same emotional intensity?
Tailgating too closely	Unilateral Blame	Did you play a role in why the person suddenly decided to tailgate you? Were you driving too slowly? Were you unresponsive to requests to move over? Did you play a role in any other way?

External Trigger	Your Brain Says "True"	What Is/May Be True
Driving too slowly	Bad/Wrong	True if driving excessively slow and no room to pass and slow driver does not eventually pull over and let others go by; False if not excessively slow but not meeting your personal standards.
Driving too slowly	Negative Impact	Being slowed down is often not a real negative impact (although sometimes it can have negative implications).
Driving too slowly	Unilateral Blame	This filter can appear to be true as it is rare that you caused someone to drive slowly (unless you did something to piss them off and they are now retaliating). But do you really know what might be causing them to drive slowly? Could they be eating while driving? Could they be old with poor vision? Could they have a severe migraine? Could they be deep in thought or be preoccupied about a sick child?

APPENDIX B: EXAMPLES OF TELLING THE TRUTH

External Trigger	Your Brain Says "True"	What Is/ May Be True
Delivery Truck Parks and Blocks Roadway	Bad/Wrong	True, it is not considerate of other drivers to knowingly block the flow of traffic; but is it reasonable to expect that everyone will always be considerate?
Delivery Truck Parks and Blocks Roadway	Negative Impact	Is it really a big deal if you have to wait 1-2 minutes before being able to proceed with your drive? Yes, it may feel like a big deal but if you are being honest, is it?
Delivery Truck Parks and Blocks Roadway	Unilateral Blame	Yes, it might appear that you had nothing to do with this. But do you ever order things to be delivered? Think about all the people ordering deliveries that put more and more trucks on the road and create greater time pressures to get everything delivered on time? And do you ever complain when things aren't delivered to you timely? Have you ever worked as a delivery driver to know what pressures and stresses they face?

These are just a few examples of what it might look like to "debate" your brain whenever it is making you angry. None of these examples is completely flushed out, and you might be able to identify other truths that I didn't mention. Also, you might not agree with every point that I made. My goal is to just give you a taste of what arguing with your brain might look and feel like. Now, go out and start practicing this anger-busting skill of arguing with your brain on your own.

About The Author

Dr. Mort Orman, M.D. is an Internal Medicine physician, a 40-year anger and stress elimination expert, and a leading transformational life mastery coach. After discovering how to cure his own anger, stress, and relationship problems as a young professional, he has been writing, teaching, and speaking on these and other health and wellness topics for decades. Dr. Orman excels at helping people pinpoint the internal causes of their problems, which are specific thoughts, beliefs, and behavior patterns that are usually invisible, so they can begin to address these internal factors and achieve victory over them.

Dr. Orman has written 26 books on eliminating anger and stress, in addition to authoring numerous online courses, articles, and self-help guides. He has also conducted hundreds of anger elimination and stress elimination workshops for doctors, nurses, medical students, veterinarians, business owners, corporate executives, the clergy, and even the F.B.I.

Dr. Orman was born and raised in Baltimore, Maryland, where he grew up idolizing legendary Baltimore Colts Hall of Fame quarterback Johnny Unitas. "Johnny U. magically transported his winning attitude into me and countless other fans, and I now endeavor to transfer that same winning mindset into others."

Dr. Orman and his wife Christina, who is a leading holistic veterinarian, now live in Florida. When we go to parties and meet new people, our motto is, "We can treat anything on either end of the leash."

To find out more about Dr. Orman, his online resources, his other books and self-help guides, his latest scheduled events, and how to arrange for him to speak to your group, company, or organization, visit his website http://DocOrman.com

www.ingramcontent.com/pod-product-compliance
Lightning Source LLC
LaVergne TN
LVHW051842080426
835512LV00018B/3027